CHAMBER MUSIC
by H. VOXMAN

for
THREE WOODWINDS, Vol. II

C Flute, B♭ Clarinet, and
Bassoon or Bass Clarinet (Easy to Medium)

CONTENTS...

		Page
ADAGIO *from Divertimento IV*	Mozart	19
AIR	Couperin	3
AMERICAN FOLK SUITE	Arr. by R. Hervig	11
ANDANTE	Handel	24
ANDANTE *from Trio in G*	Haydn	30
CHRISTMAS EVE	Arr. by R. Hervig	20
COUNTRY DANCE No. 1	Beethoven	15
FINALE *from Trio in C*	Haydn	28
GERMAN DANCE	von Weber	22
I PRAISE THEE, LORD *A Chorale for Tuning Octaves*	Bach	2
LARGHETTO *from Divertimento in B♭, Op. 12a*	Kotschau	6
MENUET	Schubert	26
MENUETTO	Haydn	16
O TOBIAS! *Canon*	Beethoven	27
PASSEPIED *from Suite in C*	Bach	14
SARABANDE AND CORRENTE	Corelli	4
TRIO No. 1 *from Brandenburg Concerto No. 1*	Bach	32
TWO GERMAN DANCES	Mozart	8
WALTZ IN D	Beethoven	29

®RUBANK. INC.

HAL•LEONARD®
CORPORATION
7777 W. BLUEMOUND RD. P.O. BOX 13819 MILWAUKEE, WI 53213

I Praise Thee, Lord
A Chorale for Tuning Octaves

Woodwind Trio*

BACH

* **NOTE:** An Oboe may be used in place of the C Flute in many of the trios in this collection.

Air

Woodwind Trio

COUPERIN

Sarabande and Corrente

Woodwind Trio

CORELLI

Woodwind Trio

Larghetto
from Divertimento in B♭, Op. 12a

KOTSCHAU

Two German Dances

I

Woodwind Trio

MOZART

II

Woodwind Trio

American Folk Suite

Woodwind Trio

Arr. by R. Hervig

Woodwind Trio

Passepied
from Suite in C

Woodwind Trio

BACH

Country Dance No.1

BEETHOVEN

Menuetto

Woodwind Trio

HAYDN

Woodwind Trio

Adagio
from Divertimento IV

Woodwind Trio

MOZART

Christmas Eve

Woodwind Trio

Arr. by R. Hervig

Woodwind Trio

O COME, ALL YE FAITHFUL

Resolutely

German Dance

von WEBER

Lively

Andante

Woodwind Trio

HANDEL

Menuet

Woodwind Trio

SCHUBERT

O Tobias!

Canon

BEETHOVEN

Finale

from Trio in C

Woodwind Trio

HAYDN

Waltz in D

BEETHOVEN

Andante
from Trio in G

Woodwind Trio

HAYDN

Trio No.1
from Brandenburg Concerto No.1

Woodwind Trio

BACH